CANTABILE – THE LONDON QUARTET

# THE GREAT BRITISH
## A CAPPELLA SONGBOOK

## PETERS EDITION LTD

A member of the EDITION PETERS GROUP
FRANKFURT/M. · LEIPZIG · LONDON · NEW YORK

Cantabile – The London Quartet
is managed by

ARTIST MANAGEMENT

Peters Edition Limited
2–6 Baches Street
London
N1 6DN
Tel: +44 (0)20 7553 4000
Fax: +44 (0)20 7490 4921
Email: sales@editionpeters.com
Internet: www.editionpeters.com

# CONTENTS

# Foreword

We are delighted that some of our arrangements, hitherto gathering dust on our shelves, have now been published. During the 35 years that we have been singing together we have built up quite a library, the vast part of which pre-dates computerized scores. It is very exciting that Edition Peters were ready to contemplate turning the torn manuscript paper, parchment and papyrus into something legible and, we hope, singable.

Appearing in this Diamond Jubilee year, when we all have had in mind what being British is all about, we thought our first collection of arrangements should reflect this, and so we have sought to choose a range of music from and about London and the British Isles.

We couldn't begin to count the number of times someone has come up to us after a concert, or written to us, to ask whether any of our music was published and available. Now that person should be satisfied, and we hope there may be a few others, too, who might enjoy singing these songs as much as we do.

The London Quartet comprises countertenor, two tenors and a baritone. In preparing this edition for soprano, alto, tenor and bass we have sought, wherever possible, to keep both to the spirit and to the letter of our own scores. In most cases, the pieces in this collection could be sung by an all male-voice group with no more change than to choose a lower key, or with some judicious octave- or part-swapping; here and there we have indicated where choices can be made. If you would like to know exactly what we do, our original versions can be downloaded from www.choralstore.com. Further information on the songs can be found at www.thelondonquartet.com.

Cantabile – The London Quartet
London, September 2012

# Vorwort

Wir freuen uns sehr über das Erscheinen des vorliegenden Bandes mit einer Auswahl unserer Arrangements, auch wenn uns bewusst ist, dass wir dieses Unterfangen vielleicht schon ein wenig eher hätten in Angriff nehmen können. Seit 35 Jahren singen wir jetzt gemeinsam, und in dieser Zeit hat sich ein beträchtliches Repertoire angesammelt, das bisher im Regal vor sich hin staubte und das überwiegend vor dem Zeitalter des Computer-Notensatzes entstand. Dass die Edition Peters sich mit dem Gedanken anfreunden konnte, unsere handgeschriebenen Papyrus-, Pergament- und Papierfetzen in etwas Lesbares – und hoffentlich Singbares – zu verwandeln, ist ein aufregender und wunderbarer Schritt.

Das Jahr 2012, in dem unsere erste Sammlung von Arrangements nun erscheint, war für uns Briten ein ganz besonderes Jahr, konnten wir doch das 60. Thronjubiläum von Königin Elisabeth II. feiern. Aus diesem Anlass haben wir eine Reihe von Werken ausgewählt, die von London und den britischen Inseln handeln oder hier entstanden.

Wir haben aufgehört zu zählen, wie oft nach unseren Konzerten jemand auf uns zukommt oder uns schreibt, um sich zu erkundigen, ob unsere Stücke im Druck erschienen und im Handel erhältlich sind. Dieser Jemand kann jetzt aufatmen, und wir hoffen, dass es auch darüber hinaus noch die eine oder andere Sängergruppe gibt, der es genauso viel Freude macht wie uns, dieses Repertoire zu singen.

Das London Quartet besteht aus Countertenor, zwei Tenören und Bariton. Beim Einrichten der vorliegenden Ausgabe für Sopran, Alt, Tenor und Bass haben wir versucht, Charakter und Notentext unserer Originalfassungen so weit wie möglich beizubehalten. Die meisten Stücke dieser Sammlung lassen sich auch von einem reinen Männerensemble singen; dazu genügt es, eine tiefere Tonart zu wählen oder einzelne Stimmen hier und dort behutsam zu tauschen oder zu oktavieren. Vereinzelt haben wir auch gekennzeichnet, wo Alternativen möglich sind. Unsere eigenen Versionen lassen sich zum Vergleich bei www.choralstore.com herunterladen, und nähere Informationen zu den Stücken sind unter www.thelondonquartet.com verfügbar.

Cantabile – The London Quartet

London, im September 2012

# About the songs

**Pastime with Good Company**                                    King Henry VIII of England (1491–1547)

Henry, as the second son of Henry VII, did not expect to be king, and so did not have the high-pressure childhood of his older brother Arthur, who should have been king. Perhaps this is why, after the unexpected death of his brother, King Henry VIII's skill as a poet and composer would seem to be greater than your average King of England. Not that his fighting, hunting and partying were anything but excellent...

This piece is in the British Library as part of the Henry VIII manuscript (c.1513), with 13 other works, signed 'by the King's hand'.

**Greensleeves**                    Traditional English; words from *A Handful of Pleasant Delights* (1584)

Delightful as it would be to say that this, like 'Pastime with Good Company', was composed by Henry VIII, it appears that the Italian verse form in which it is written did not arrive in England until years after Henry's death. First mentioned in the 1580s, it is an Elizabethan tune (Elizabeth I reigned 1558–1603). While there are many more verses, we consider these four to be the most beautiful.

**Oranges and Lemons**                                                        Traditional English

This traditional English nursery rhyme mentions the bells of many of London's churches. It was first printed in *Tommy Thumb's Pretty Songbook* around 1744; a dance entitled 'Oranges and Lemons' also appeared in 1665 in Playford's *Dancing Master*, but it is not clear that the two versions are linked. The bells mentioned in the song were all, it seems, in and around the City of London (now London's financial district), although it is not certain exactly which churches the song refers to. Here are the best ideas:

- St Clement's: St Clement Danes or St Clement Eastcheap (both near the wharves where citrus fruits were landed in the Port of London)
- St Martin's: St Martin Ongar or St Martin's Lane (both in the City, where moneylenders lived)
- Old Bailey: St Sepulchre-without-Newgate (opposite The Old Bailey – the Central Criminal Court for England and Wales, near the old Fleet Prison where debtors were held)
- Shoreditch: St Leonard's, Shoreditch (just outside the City walls)
- Stepney: St Dunstan's, Stepney (also just outside the City walls)
- Bow (pronounced as in 'bow and arrow'): St Mary-le-Bow in Cheapside

'Oranges and Lemons' has also – erroneously – been linked with the ubiquitous Henry VIII. It has been supposed that it refers to his six wives – but the truth would seem to be that it was written at different times, and earlier versions of the poem mention more than six bells!

**Myfanwy**                    Joseph Parry (1841–1903); words by Mynyddog (Richard Davies) (1833–1877)

'Scratch any Welshman,' it is said, 'and he will sing' – and as likely as not he will sing 'Myfanwy', this simple but beautiful iconic anthem to love lost. Its composer, Joseph Parry, lived for a number of years in the USA, and indeed he used the name 'Pencerdd America'. The author of the poem, Mynyddog (the bardic name of Richard Davies), could not have chosen a more Welsh subject: Myfanwy, a name which conjures up various legends; indeed Parry's own childhood sweetheart was called Myfanwy. Another of Parry's tunes, 'Aberystwyth' was used in South Africa's national anthem, 'Nkosi Sikelel' iAfrika'.

**Danny Boy ('I would be true')**

Traditional Irish;
words by Frederic E. Weatherly (1848–1929)
and Howard Walter (1883–1918)

This tune, 'Londonderry Air', is an old Irish melody. Many different lyrics have been added to it: we provide two in this setting. The words by Frederic Weatherly, an English lawyer, lyricist and author, are perhaps the most well-known. The words by Howard Walter, written in 1906, are famous for having been performed at the funeral of Diana, Princess of Wales in 1997.

**A Man's a Man for A' That**

Traditional Scottish ('Lady McIntosh's Reel');
words by Robert Burns (1759–1796)

Robert Burns is the national poet of Scotland. Known to be a supporter of both the American and French revolutions, perhaps he had in mind Thomas Paine's recent *The Rights of Man* (1791) when he wrote this poem in 1795. The song was sung at the re-opening of Scottish Parliament in 1999 and at the funeral of the inaugural First Minister of Scotland, Donald Dewar, in 2000.

**Pomp and Circumstance**

Edward Elgar (1857–1934);
words by Margarete and Julian Forsyth

When creating our *Best of British* show for German and subsequently Belgian theatres, we needed a stirring piece of patriotic music, but with suitably self-deprecating words. We decided that Elgar's *Pomp and Circumstance March No. 4* would be the best tune for this purpose (although the more famous tune, 'Land of Hope and Glory', from *March No. 1* is included here to introduce it). When it came to the lyrics, we approached the wonderfully creative Maggie and Julian Forsyth (a great couple – both directors, translators, writers and actors); they concocted a fabulous list of things British.

**A Foggy Day**

George Gershwin (1898–1937);
words by Ira Gershwin (1896–1983)

'A Foggy Day' was first sung by Fred Astaire in the 1937 film, *A Damsel in Distress*. It was originally entitled 'A Foggy Day (In London Town)': a great American composer's take on our great capital city – listen out for the Westminster Chimes of London's Big Ben. We wrote this arrangement in tribute to Gene Puerling, who kindly encouraged us in our writing. He was the master of four-part male-voice jazz arrangements – nothing surpasses his own vocal group, the Hi-Lo's.

**Lullaby (Hush Macushla)**

Cantabile – The London Quartet

'Macushla' is a transliteration of part of the Irish phrase, *a chuisle mo chroí* ('my heart's pulse'), and thus *mo chuisle* means 'darling' or 'sweetheart'. When we chose to put an original song on our CD *Lullabyes and Goodbyes*, our own tenor, Mark Fleming, who remembered the rhyming title from when he was very small, came up with this lullaby, which immediately had the other three of us under its spell.

# Über die Stücke

### Pastime with Good Company
Heinrich VIII. von England (1491–1547)

Als zweitältester Sohn von Heinrich VII. konnte Heinrich VIII. nicht damit rechnen, einmal König zu werden. Im Gegensatz zu seinem älteren Bruder Arthur, der den Thron erben sollte, verlebte er daher eine recht unbeschwerte Kindheit. Vielleicht ist dies der Grund, warum König Heinrich VIII. nach dem unerwarteten Tod seines Bruders größeres Talent zum Dichten und Komponieren an den Tag legte, als man es von englischen Königen im Allgemeinen gewohnt war. Wobei seine Begabung zum Kämpfen, Jagen und Feiern natürlich völlig außer Frage steht …

Zusammen mit dreizehn anderen Werken bildet das Stück die Handschrift Heinrichs VIII. (ca. 1513), die sich in der British Library befindet und den Hinweis „By the King's Hand" trägt.

### Greensleeves
Englische Volksweise; Text aus *A Handful of Pleasant Delights* (1584)

So schön es auch wäre zu behaupten, dass dieses Stück ebenso aus der Feder von Heinrich VIII. stammt wie „Pastime with Good Company", scheint die zugrunde liegende italienische Gedichtform doch erst einige Jahre nach Heinrichs Tod bis nach England vorgedrungen zu sein. Erwähnt wird das Werk erstmals in den 1580er Jahren, es handelt sich also um ein Lied aus der elisabethanischen Zeit (Elisabeth I. regierte von 1558 bis 1603). Es existiert noch eine ganze Reihe weiterer Strophen, doch die vier hier ausgewählten sind unserer Ansicht nach die schönsten.

### Oranges and Lemons
Englische Volksweise

In diesem traditionellen englischen Kinderreim werden die Glockenklänge mehrerer Londoner Kirchen aufgezählt. Gedruckt erschien das Stück erstmals um 1744 in *Tommy Thumb's Pretty Songbook*; ein Tanz mit dem Titel „Oranges and Lemons" findet sich auch in John Playfords *Dancing Master* von 1655, wobei jedoch unklar ist, ob zwischen den beiden Fassungen eine Verbindung besteht. Die im Lied erwähnten Glockengeläute scheinen sämtlich aus der City of London (dem heutigen Finanzdistrikt) und aus der unmittelbaren Umgebung zu stammen, wenn auch nicht sicher ist, um welche Kirchen es sich handelt. Am wahrscheinlichsten sind folgende Möglichkeiten:

- St. Clement's: St. Clement Danes oder St. Clement Eastcheap (beide in der Nähe der Kais, an denen im Londoner Hafen die Zitrusfrüchte angelandet wurden)
- St. Martin's: St. Martin Ongar oder St. Martin's Lane (beide im Geldverleiher-Viertel der City)
- Old Bailey: St. Sepulchre-without-Newgate (gegenüber von „Old Bailey", dem Zentralen Strafgerichtshof von England and Wales, in der Nähe des ehemaligen Fleet Prison, wo säumige Schuldner inhaftiert wurden)
- Shoreditch: St. Leonard's, Shoreditch (direkt vor den Mauern der City)
- Stepney: St. Dunstan's, Stepney (ebenfalls direkt vor der Stadtmauer)
- Bow (gesprochen wie „low"): St Mary-le-Bow im Stadtviertel Cheapside

Auch *Oranges and Lemons* wurde fälschlich dem umtriebigen Heinrich VIII. zugeschrieben. Man sah darin einen Hinweis auf seine sechs Frauen – in Wirklichkeit scheint das Lied jedoch nach und nach entstanden zu sein, und in frühen Fassungen des Gedichts kommen mehr als sechs Kirchengeläute vor!

### Myfanwy
Joseph Parry (1841–1903); Text von Mynyddog (Richard Davies) (1833–1877)

Einem englischen Sprichwort zufolge muss man an einem Waliser nur kratzen, schon fängt er an zu singen – und höchstwahrscheinlich bringt er dann „Myfanwy" zu Gehör, ein schlichtes, aber herrliches Lied über verlorene Liebe, das in Wales großen Symbolwert hat. Der Komponist, Joseph Parry, lebte etliche Jahre in den USA und verwendete sogar als Pseudonym den Namen „Pencerdd America". Autor des Gedichttexts war der „Barde" Mynyddog (Richard Davies), und er hätte kaum einen anderen Stoff finden können, der so eng mit Wales verbunden ist: Der Mädchenname Myfanwy erinnert an eine Vielzahl von Sagen und Legenden – und auch die erste Jugendliebe des Komponisten selbst hieß Myfanwy. Ein anderes Werk aus Parrys Feder, „Aberystwyth", ist heute Teil der südafrikanischen Nationalhymne „Nkosi Sikelel' iAfrika".

### Danny Boy („I would be true")

Irische Volksweise;
Text von Frederic E. Weatherly (1848–1929)
und Howard Walter (1883–1918)

Bei dieser Melodie, „Londonderry Air", handelt es sich um eine alte irische Volksweise. Viele verschiedene Texte wurden dazu gesungen; in unserem Arrangement verwenden wir zwei davon. Wohl am bekanntesten sind die Verse von Frederic Weatherly, einem englischen Juristen, Dichter und Schriftsteller, während der 1906 entstandene Text von Howard Walter durch seine Verwendung beim Begräbnis von Prinzessin Diana im Jahr 1997 zu Berühmtheit gelangte.

### A Man's a Man for A' That

Schottische Volksweise (Lady McIntosh's Reel);
Text von Robert Burns (1759–1796)

Robert Burns ist Schottlands Nationaldichter. Es ist bekannt, dass er Anhänger der Revolutionen in Amerika und Frankreich war, und als solcher hatte er vielleicht Thomas Paines einige Jahre zuvor entstandenes Buch *The Rights of Man* (1791) im Sinn, als er 1795 dieses Gedicht schrieb. Das Lied erklang 1999 bei der Eröffnung des wiedergegründeten schottischen Parlaments sowie beim Begräbnis des im Jahr 2000 verstorbenen ersten schottischen Ministerpräsidenten, Donald Dewar.

### Pomp and Circumstance

Edward Elgar (1857–1934),
Text von Margarete und Julian Forsyth

Bei der Vorbereitung unseres Programms *Best of British*, mit dem wir zunächst in Deutschland, dann in Belgien auf Tournee waren, brauchten wir ein Stück mit ergreifend patriotischer Musik, das zum Ausgleich aber einen eher selbstironischen Text haben sollte. Wir beschlossen, dass der Marsch Nr. 4 aus Elgars *Pomp and Circumstance* sich am besten als Melodie eignen würde (während die bekanntere Weise „Land of Hope and Glory" aus dem Marsch Nr. 1 hier als Einleitung erklingt). Mit Blick auf den Text wandten wir uns an das wunderbar kreative Duo Maggie und Julian Forsyth (beide sind als Regisseure, Übersetzer, Schriftsteller und Schauspieler tätig), und sie lieferten uns eine fabelhafte Liste all dessen, was typisch britisch ist.

### A Foggy Day

George Gershwin (1898–1937);
Text von Ira Gershwin (1896–1983)

„A Foggy Day" war erstmals 1937 in dem Film *A Damsel in Distress* („Ein Fräulein in Nöten") zu hören, gesungen von Fred Astaire. Ursprünglich lautete der Titel des Stücks „A Foggy Day (In London Town)": Der berühmte amerikanische Komponist blickt hier auf die berühmte englische Hauptstadt – man achte auf den Glockenschlag von Big Ben. Unser Arrangement entstand als Hommage an Gene Puerling, der uns in unserer Arbeit freundlich ermutigte. Er war der unbestrittene Meister des vierstimmigen Jazzarrangements für Männerstimmen – und seine eigene Vokalgruppe, The Hi-Lo's, bleibt unübertroffen.

### Lullaby (Hush Macushla)

Cantabile – The London Quartet

„Macushla" ist eine lautschriftliche Übertragung, die sich vom irischen Ausdruck „a chuisle mo chroí" („meines Herzens Schlag") ableitet; „mo chuisle" bedeutet also „mein Herz" oder „mein Liebling". Nachdem wir beschlossen hatten, für unser Album *Lullabyes and Goodbyes* auch ein eigenes Stück aufzunehmen, erinnerte sich unser Tenor Mark Fleming an diese gereimte Wendung aus seiner Kindheit und dachte sich das hier abgedruckte Schlaflied aus, das uns alle sofort in seinen Bann zog.

# Pastime with Good Company

from the album *In Cambridge*

King Henry VIII of England
Arranged by Cantabile – The London Quartet

*gruch: (be)grudge

We have changed one note from the original manuscript: in bar 22 the last note in the tenor line is a low F; we prefer the more chunky parallel fifths which result from singing an A. The optional descant is not in the original.

# Greensleeves

A *Handful of Pleasant Delights* (1584)

Traditional English
Arranged by Cantabile – The London Quartet

Note: the tune changes from the first half to the second – C♭s and C♮s all as marked.

Green - sleeves was my de - light, Green - sleeves was my heart of gold, And who but la - dy Green - sleeves

Oo_____ Oo_____

have been rea - dy   at your hand, to grant what-e - ver thou would'st crave, I  have both wa - ged life and land, your
(you would)

Oo_____ Oo_____

Oo_____ Oo_____

Thou could'st de - sire___ no earth - ly thing,_ But still thou hadst_ it
(You could)                                              (you had)

read - i - ly, Thy mu - sic still___ to play and sing,_ And yet___ thou would'st not
(Your)                                                          (you would)

# Oranges and Lemons

Traditional English
Arranged by Cantabile – The London Quartet

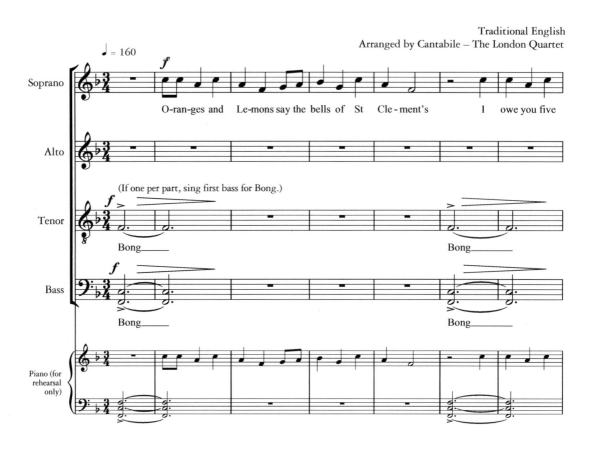

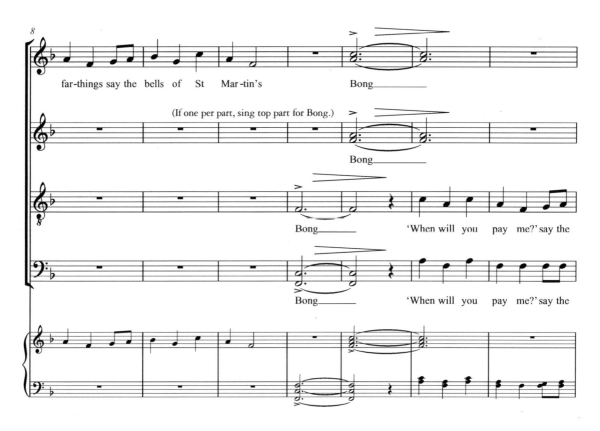

# Myfanwy

Mynyddog (bardic name of Richard Davies)

Dr Joseph Parry
Arranged by Cantabile – The London Quartet

\* Original Welsh lyrics

NB: See page 72 for the Welsh lyrics pronunciation guide.

wish no more your hand, My-fan-wy, If I no lon-ger have your heart.
fy - naf byth mo'th law, My-fan-wy, Heb gael dy ga-lon gy-da hi.

wish no more your hand, My-fan-wy, If I no lon-ger have your heart.
fy - naf byth mo'th law, My-fan-wy, Heb gael dy ga-lon gy-da hi.

wish no more your hand, My-fan-wy, If I no lon-ger have your heart.
fy - naf byth mo'th law, My-fan-wy, Heb gael dy ga-lon gy-da hi.

wish no more your hand, My-fan-wy, If I no lon-ger have your heart. My -
fy - naf byth mo'th law, My-fan-wy, Heb gael dy ga-lon gy-da hi. My -

Mm

Mm

Mm

- fan - wy may you spend your life-time Be - neath the mid - day sun-shine's glow,_ And
- fan - wy, boed yr oll o'th fy-wyd, Dân heul - wen ddys-glaer ca - nol dydd;_ A

Bass II
(optional)

Mm

* If no Bass II available, please sing the D.

# Danny Boy

### 'I would be true'

#### (Londonderry Air)

Frederick E. Weatherly,
Howard A. Walter ('I would be true')

Traditional Irish
Arranged by Cantabile – The London Quartet

The two lines of lyrics represent the two versions of the text and are alternatives rather than first and second verses.

# A Man's a Man for A' That

Robert Burns

Traditional Scottish
Arranged by Cantabile – The London Quartet

44

a': *all*

hoddin grey: *homemade, rough cloth*

coof: *idiot*

maunna fa' that: *may / must not do that*

bear the gree: *win the victory*

gowd: *gold*

birkie: *an arrogant man*

aboon: *above*

pith: *strength / force*

# Pomp and Circumstance

Margarete and Julian Forsyth

Edward Elgar
Arranged by Cantabile – The London Quartet

**Allegro marziale – make as grand as you wish!**

All voices, unison at appropriate pitch:

Hm

**Nobilmente (l'istesso tempo)**

104

wait-ing in a queue,_____ Ta - king tea and snacks, Wa - ving

110

Un - ion Jacks, Ev - 'ry - thing is so re - laxed; It's Bri - tish

**Grandioso**

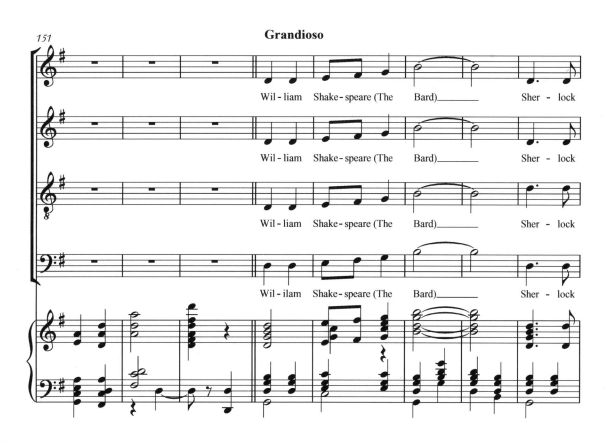

Wil - liam Shake - speare (The Bard)_____ Sher - lock

Wil - liam Shake - speare (The Bard)_____ Sher - lock

Wil - liam Shake - speare (The Bard)_____ Sher - lock

Wil - liam Shake - speare (The Bard)_____ Sher - lock

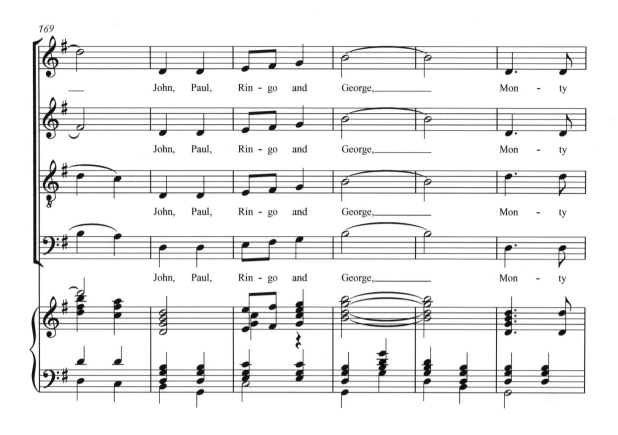

John, Paul, Rin - go and George,_____ Mon - ty

Py - thon's Sil - ly Walks,_____ Cric - ket on the green, James Bond,

\* Alternative German text for final verse.

# A Foggy Day

from the album *And Now ...*

Ira Gershwin

George Gershwin
Arranged by Cantabile – The London Quartet

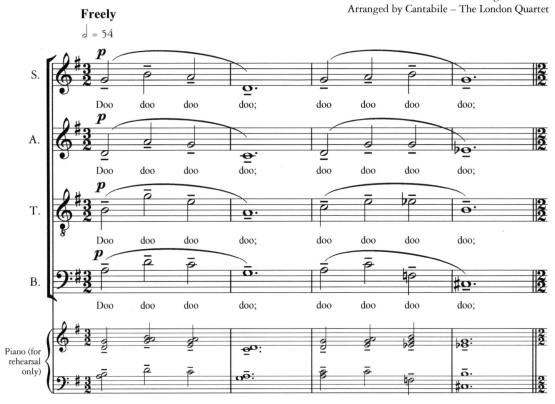

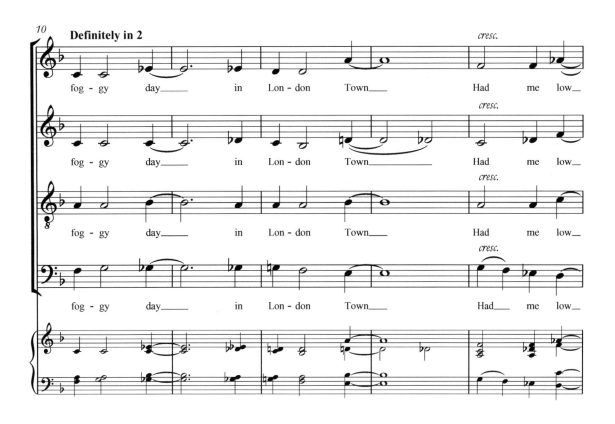

22

Bri - tish Mu - se - um had lost its charm.____

Bri - tish Mu - se - um had lost its charm.____

Bri - tish Mu - se - um had lost its charm.____

Bri - tish Mu - se - um had lost its charm.____

26 **Ease back, but fluid (straight 8s)**

I was a stran - ger in the ci - ty;____ Out of town were the

I was a stran - ger in the ci - ty;____ Out of town were the

I was a stran - ger in the ci - ty;____ Out of town were the

I was a stran - ger in the ci - ty;____ Out of town were the

peo - ple I knew;___ I had that feel - ing of self - pi - ty;___ What to

rit.

do? What to do? What to do? The out - look was de - ci - ded - ly

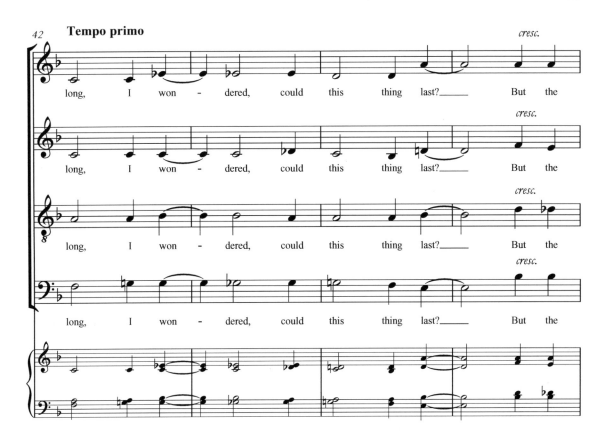

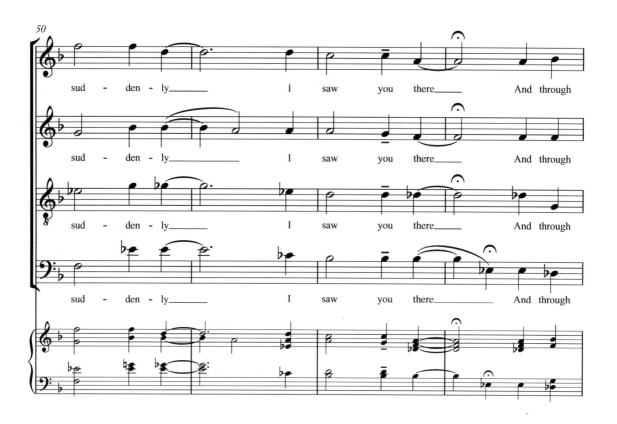

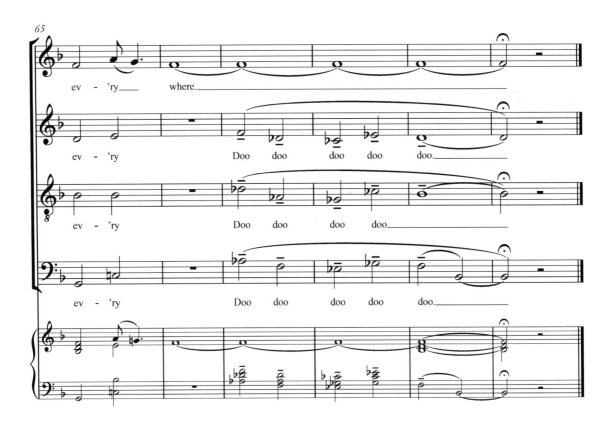

# Lullaby (Hush Macushla)

from the album *Lullabyes and Goodbyes*

Cantabile – The London Quartet

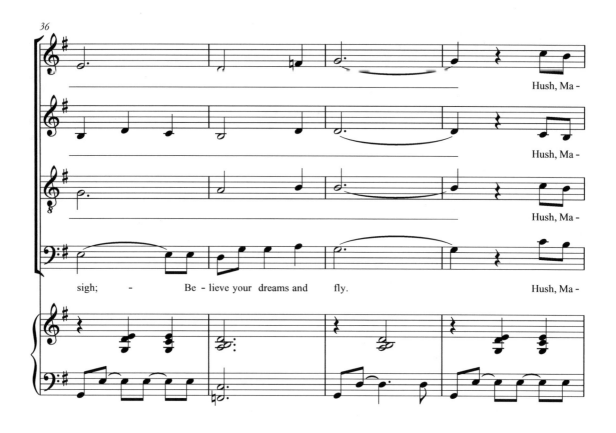

# Myfanwy – Pronuncation Guide

| | |
|---|---|
| Paham mae dicter, O Myfanwy, | pɑː-ham mai dɪk-tɛr oː mə-van-uːi |
| Yn llenwi'th lygaid duon di? | on ɬon wiθ lo gaid diː ɔn di. |
| A'th ruddiau tirion, O Myfanwy, | ɑːθ riː-ðjai ti-rjɔn oː mə-van-uːi |
| Heb wrido wrth fy ngweled i? | heb wriː-dɔ wrθ və ŋwɛ-lɛd iː |
| Pa le mae'r wên oedd ar dy wefus | pɑː le mair wen ɔið ar də we-vis |
| Fu'n cynnau 'nghariad ffyddlon ffôl? | viːn kə-nai ka-rjad fəð-lɔn foːl |
| Pa le mae sain dy eiriau melys, | pɑː le mai sain də ai-rjai mɛ-lis |
| Fu'n denu'n nghalon ar dy ôl? | vin dɛ-ni ŋa-lon ar də oːl |

| | |
|---|---|
| Pa beth a wneuthum, O Myfanwy | pɑː-beθ ɑː wnai-θim oː mə-van-uːi |
| I haeddu gwg dy ddwyrudd hardd? | iː hai-ði guːg də ðuːi-riːð harð |
| Ai chwarae oeddit, O Myfanwy | ai χwa-rair ɔi-ðit oː mə-vɑːn-uːi |
| Â thanau euraidd serch dy fardd? | ɑː θa-nai ai-raið sɛrχ də varð |
| Wyt eiddo im drwy gywir amod | uːit ai-dɔ im druːi gə-wir a-mɔd |
| Ai gormod cadw'th air i mi? | ai gɔr-mɔd ka-dwθ air iː mi |
| Ni cheisiaf fyth mo'th law, Myfanwy, | niː və-nav bɪθ mɔθ law mə-van-uːi |
| Heb gael dy galon gyda hi. | heb gail də ga-lɔn gə-da hiː |

| | |
|---|---|
| Myfanwy boed yr holl o'th fywyd | mə-van-uːi bɔid ər oɬ oːθ və-wid |
| Dan heulwen ddisglair canol dydd. | dɑːn hail-wɛn ðis-glair ca-nɔl diːð |
| A boed i rosyn gwridog iechyd | ɑː bɔid i rɔ-sin gwriː-dɔg jɛ-χid |
| I ddawnsio ganmlwydd ar dy rudd. | iː ðawn-sio gan-mluːið ar də riːð |
| Anghofia'r oll o'th addewidion | a-ŋhɔ-vjar oɬ oːθ ɑː-ðə-wi-djɔn |
| A wnest i rywun, 'ngeneth ddel, | ɑː wnəst i rɪ-win ɛ-nɛθ ðɛl |
| A dyro'th law, Myfanwy dirion | ɑː də-rɔθ law mə-van-uːi di-rjɔn |
| I ddim ond dweud y gair "Ffarwél". | iː ðim ɔnd dwaid ə gair far-wɛl |

## Notes

A sound which might be unusual to English, but not German speakers, would be the 'ch', as in the Scots 'loch' or the Yinglish 'chutzpah'.

A sound which might be unusual to most non-Welsh speakers would be the 'll', which is somewhere between the voiceless 'l' in English 'please' and the 'tl' in 'antler'. You can produce it thus: go to pronounce a letter 'l', stop as the tip of the tongue touches the roof of the mouth, and blow around the sides of the tongue.

The 'dd' (functioning in Welsh as a single letter – should always have a note going through it; pronounce it as the 'th' in the English 'this', not as in 'think'.

In this song the most important sound to get right is the last syllable of 'Myfanwy'; there is much more 'w' (English 'oo') than 'y' (English 'ee')!

There are several variants on the text of 'Myfanwy'. We have chosen the oldest generally available version (1882), with certain spellings modified to comply with modern usage. The most obvious variant one hears these days is in the second verse: 'Ni cheisiaf fyth mo'th law, Myfanwy...' for the original 'Ni fynaf byth mo'th law, Myfanwy...'. We are most grateful for the help given us in this by Tŷ Cerdd – Music Centre Wales, The National Library of Wales, Dr Gethin Matthews and Dr E. Wyn James.